One-Minute
Jewish Stories

One-Minute
Jewish Stories

Adapted by
Shari Lewis
Illustrated by Roberta Collier

Doubleday

NEW YORK LONDON TORONTO SYDNEY AUCKLAND

To my mother Ann Ritz Hurwitz,
the first Jewish storyteller in my life,
who loves a good tale as much as I do!

Acknowledgments
Religious adviser: Rabbi James Michaels of the Whitestone Hebrew Center
in New York City. Research by Sharon Eisenberg, and by Susan North of
Temple Emanuel in Los Angeles, California. And thanks to Martin Sage for
his efforts on behalf of this book.

Published by Doubleday, a division of
Bantam Doubleday Dell Publishing Group, Inc.
666 Fifth Avenue, New York, New York 10103

Doubleday and the portrayal of an anchor
with a dolphin are trademarks of Doubleday,
a division of Bantam Doubleday Dell Publishing Group, Inc.

Library of Congress Cataloging-in-Publication Data
Lewis, Shari.
One-minute Jewish stories/adapted by Shari Lewis; illustrated
by Roberta Collier.—1st ed.
p.   cm.
Summary: Twenty stories from various aspects of Jewish life—the
Talmud, folklore, the Bible, history—all in a format for reading in
one minute.
ISBN 0-385-24447-9
1. Legends, Jewish—Juvenile literature.   2. Fasts and feasts—
Judiasm—Juvenile literature.   [1. Folklore, Jewish.   2. Judaism.]
I. Collier, Roberta, ill.   II. Title.
BM530.L42 1989   88-21113
909'.04924—dc19   CIP
                                                          AC
RL: 3.3

Contents

Introduction

*G*RANDPA was a rabbi. So were Uncle Saul and Cousin Moshe. Daddy was a professor at Yeshiva University. However, he was also Official Magician for the City of New York, while Mother was one of the music coordinators for the New York City Board of Education. As a child, I was far more fascinated by the family's theatricality than by its Jewishness.

Mind you, I've always loved the traditions and reveled in a sense of connection to that extended family that embraces you not for what you do, but simply because you are a member of the tribe. But I had never delved into Jewish literature.

So I began this, my ninth "One-Minute" story book, as a *literary* exercise. It became a personally stirring experience.

As the saying goes, "A writer writes, a reader reads." In case this bit of wisdom seems too deep or too dull-witted, I'll explain: As a writer, you may think you know who you are and what the material means to you, but you can't begin to know who the reader will be, or what background that reader will or won't bring to the page.

When I started researching, I tried to visualize the reader: a Jewish-American adult, hoping to share his or her cultural heritage with a child whose frame of reference is mainly shaped by the images on the television screen. Perhaps (in this enlightened era of ethnic studies) the book would be in the hands of a non-Jewish parent or teacher interested in broadening the youngster's knowledge to include cross-cultural information.

What I hadn't calculated was the emotional impact that immersing myself in these simple stories of Jewish life would have on *me*. After all, I'd been casually exposed to this material many times before. It had never touched me, pained me, thrilled me, inspired me. This time, I was ready.

I found myself weeping as I read of the indomitable spirit with which endless generations of Jews have faced a hostile world. I was calmed by the continuing traditions, and elated by the strength of the Jewish people's faith not only in God, but also in one another. And my greatest delight was in the humor with which they kept bitterness at bay.

In the course of my research, I interviewed many Jewish scholars, rabbis, and Sunday school teachers. The consensus was this: Like me, there are many Jewish-American children who are not particularly interested in their heritage because they were never introduced to the material in a way that engaged their imaginations, stimulated their emotions, and tickled their funnybones.

And, of course, there's always been the time factor: Even in childhood, there are so many distractions vying for our free moments!

I was encouraged (by the scholars, rabbis, and teachers) to adapt these classic tales to the "One-Minute" form in order to create a smorgasbord of stories, providing youngsters with a tasty sampling of the many flavors of Jewish life and literature.

Focusing on the tradition rather than the religion, I personally savor those stories that are loosely based on historical figures (like Hertzl). But even the stories that are clearly not true represent very personal Jewish mythology. In some way, I feel that these legendary events are all the more real for their exaggeration. I hope you'll be able to enjoy even the most fanciful of these Jewish fables as bigger than life, but somehow not make-believe.

Shari Lewis

Why the Moon Is Smaller Than the Sun

*I*T is said that when God first created the universe, He made the Sun and the Moon equal in size and brightness, with equal power to light the Earth.

But the Moon complained to God, "Why should the Sun be as big as I? I'd like you to take away some of the Sun's brightness, so *I* can rule the sky."

God was very sad. His new, perfect universe was already clouded with selfishness.

"You must be punished for your vanity!" He roared. "I'm going to make you tiny compared to the Sun."

And with that, God pulled off several layers of the Moon's glowing crust, and out of that crust He made billions of glittering stars.

"Now you'll get your light only from the glimmer of the Sun and the stars. That should teach you a lesson!"

But when the Moon cried and begged forgiveness, the merciful God made a comforting promise: "These stars will never leave your side, and the Jewish people will forever trace their days, weeks, and years by *your* rise and fall in the heavens."

And although most people measure time by the Sun, to this day the Jewish calendar is based on the comings and goings of the Moon.

How Abraham Came to Believe in Just One God

WHEN Abraham was born, people still worshipped stars or stones or animals, and gave no thought to there being just one God.

As a boy, Abraham had to hide in a cave with his father Terah. Because King Nimrod had been told that the Jews who would be Abraham's children would take over Nimrod's kingdom, the King wanted to kill Abraham.

For years, tucked away in that cave, Abraham did not see the light of day.

When he finally set eyes on the sun, he exclaimed, "This much light can only be coming from the ruler of the whole world!"

But the sun set, and its heavenly place was filled by the moon and stars. Then Abraham was sure the tiny moon was even mightier, for it was surrounded by its thousands of servants, the stars.

At daybreak Abraham was shocked to see the sun once more take the moon's place.

"Strange," he thought, "that such great lights should be forced to take turns in the sky. Neither would go away if some greater power weren't *insisting* that they leave. That single mighty Being, who can't be seen, must be the ruler of the whole world!"

Abraham and the Idols

*A*BRAHAM'S father, Terah, used molds to make idols out of clay, to sell in his shop. Terah believed that these statues were gods, so he prayed to them and asked them for favors. Abraham felt that these idols were nothing special, for Abraham was convinced that there was just one true God.

One day, Terah put Abraham in charge of the shop. Then Terah went away on a trip. A man came in asking to buy an idol.

"How old are you?" asked Abraham.

"Sixty," replied the man.

Abraham laughed. "If you are sixty years old, how could you worship an idol that is just *one day* old?"

Confused, the man left without buying anything.

Later a woman brought a bowl of flour to offer to the idols. "Can a piece of clay eat?" cried Abraham. And with that, he smashed all but the largest idol.

When his father returned and saw the mess, Abraham said, "A woman brought flour as an offering, but when the idols saw it, they began to fight, and only the biggest statue survived. The flour was spilled, so even that idol didn't get any. Should I see if he's still hungry?"

Terah yelled, "You're lying! How can an idol that *I* made with my own hands *fight*, or be *hungry*?"

"I agree," said Abraham. "Your idols can neither hear, eat, nor get angry. They are lumps of clay. How can *you* worship them?"

And from then on, Abraham made no secret of his belief in one true God.

How Moses Became a Stutterer

PHARAOH'S daughter found Moses in the river and brought the baby to the palace.

One day, as Pharaoh was playing with little Moses, the baby grabbed Pharaoh's crown and placed it on his own tiny head. Everyone was horrified!

"That child will someday rob you of your crown," cried one of Pharaoh's advisers. "Moses must be killed."

"I have a better idea," said another. "Put two bowls in front of the boy, one filled with brightly colored jewels, the other with burning embers. If the boy is going to take your crown, he will reach for the jewels. Then he'll *deserve* to die."

Pharaoh agreed.

So baby Moses was placed in front of the two bowls. He happily began to reach for the shiny jewels, but God had the angel Gabriel swoop down and push Moses' hand into the hot coals. God knew that Moses would grow up to lead His people, so it was important that Moses not be killed!

Well, the hot coals burned baby Moses' hand, and he stuck his fingers into his mouth to cool them—only to burn his tongue on a fiery ember still stuck to the tip of a finger.

God had saved Moses' life, but from the day he burned his tongue to the day he died, Moses stuttered when he spoke.

David and the Spider's Web

$\mathcal{W}$HEN King David was still a shepherd boy, he often watched with wonder as spiders spun their webs across branches of nearby bushes. One day David asked the wisest man in the village, "Why did God create spiders? You can't even make cloth from the webs they weave."

The learned man answered, "None of God's creatures are useless. Someday you will thank God for the spider."

Well, David became famous for killing the giant Goliath, and married King Saul's daughter. But when Saul became angry with him and tried to kill David, he fled and hid in a cave. A big spider quickly wove a web across the opening of the cave.

That night Saul and his soldiers passed the cave. One shouted, "I'll bet David is hiding in there."

"Not possible," Saul replied. "See that spiderweb stretching across the entrance of the cave? David couldn't have gotten in without ripping the web."

So King Saul and his soldiers went away. And as the wise man had said he would, David thanked God for creating the spider.

The Site of the Temple

KING Solomon wanted to build his great temple honoring God in the holiest spot in Israel.

One night Solomon took a walk. Suddenly he saw a man carry an armload of wheat to a neighboring field, and then come back for more. He did this till the first field was empty. Then the man crept away. "A thief," thought Solomon.

Suddenly a second man appeared in the neighboring field, picked up an armload of wheat, and did the same thing as the first man, except this one carried the wheat back to the first field!

The next day Solomon called the first man to him and asked, "Why did you steal from your neighbor?"

"That neighbor's my brother," this first man insisted. "He has a large family, while I am single. My brother needs more wheat than I, but would never accept any from me. I carry the wheat to him in secret. I can do without."

Solomon then called the other brother before him and asked the same question. "My family helps me in the field," said this brother. "My brother is alone and has to *hire* help. He needs *more* wheat to sell, so he can pay the people he hires. He won't *take* wheat from me, so I *give* it to him, on the sly."

Solomon brought the brothers together.

"Forgive me for thinking you were thieves. Sell me your fields," begged Solomon, "for they are holy with brotherly love. There's no finer place to build a temple of God."

Solomon and the Baby Bee

ONE sunny day, as King Solomon slept under a big fig tree a tiny bee bit him smack on the end of his nose. Solomon awoke in pain, his nose swelling and reddening like a ripe plum. "How could you do this? Aren't you afraid of the anger of the king?"

The bee stammered, "I'm just a baby bee, and I haven't learned the difference between a nose and a flower. Your nose smelled like a flower and was as pretty as an apple. I thought I'd take a taste. Do me a favor. Forgive me. Someday I'll do you a favor too!" The king laughed at the idea that he might need the help of a tiny insect, and the baby bee flew away.

Years later, the Queen of Sheba brought gifts to Solomon, and riddles to test his wisdom.

She spread lots of flowers on the ground, saying, "Most of these were made by skilled craftsmen. Only one flower is real. Which one is it?" Solomon was stumped. They all looked alike. But when a tiny bee landed on one of the blossoms, he pointed and said, "That's the live flower!"

And that was when Solomon learned that even the mightiest of kings can be helped by the tiniest of bees.

Solomon added to his book of proverbs: "Whoso despiseth any of God's creatures shall suffer thereby."

The Story of Purim

MORDECAI raised his cousin, a smart and beautiful Jewish girl named Esther. When she was grown she married King Ahasuerus, who didn't know that she was Jewish, or that Mordecai was her cousin. One day, entering the palace to visit Queen Esther, Mordecai overheard servants plotting to kill the king. He told Esther, who informed the king, and the servants were punished.

Now this king's adviser was Haman, a nasty man who forced everybody to bow down to him. Mordecai refused, saying, "I'm a Jew. I bow only to God."

That's when Haman decided to kill not only Mordecai, but all the Jews in the kingdom!

So Esther gave a big party. She invited the king, Haman, and Mordecai as well.

At the party Esther asked the king, "Would you grant me one wish?" He agreed. Then Esther told him that *she* was Jewish, that Haman was going to kill all her people, and she asked the king to stop the massacre.

At that, the king ordered *Haman* to be killed, and Purim is the happy holiday that celebrates the time when Queen Esther saved her people.

The Festival of Lights: Hanukkah

WHAT YOU SHOULD KNOW BEFORE
READING THIS STORY:

The biggest, most holy temple the Jews
ever had was the one in Jerusalem, more
than two thousand years ago. In it were
holy books and precious objects, including
a big golden menorah (a lamp with nine
branches) which could only be lit with
the purest olive oil. The important
thing was that the lights in the menorah
burned every day and were never allowed
to go out.

*W*HEN the King of Syria, Antiochus, invaded the land of Israel, his army took over the great temple and ruled the city of Jerusalem. He killed Jews if they prayed or studied Torah, celebrated Jewish holidays, or practiced Jewish customs.

But even though his army was much bigger, a small band of brave Jews led by Judah Maccabee finally pushed Antiochus' men out of Jerusalem.

At the holy temple, Judah Maccabee was saddened to see a stone idol standing in the holiest place, and most of the precious things smashed or stolen.

They cleaned the temple, and wanted to have a rededication ceremony, called a Hanukkah. They needed to light the menorah, but could find only enough pure oil to last for one day. However, that bit of oil burned for eight days, giving them time to prepare *more* new oil.

It was a miracle, and ever since, at Hanukkah, Jews light oil or candles in a menorah each night for eight days, to celebrate the Festival of Lights.

Jonah and the Tree

*G*OD ordered Jonah to warn the wicked people in the city
of Nineveh that if they didn't behave and ask forgiveness,
God would destroy them.

But Jonah found the people there to be so wicked, he shouted
toward the heavens, "God, these people aren't worth saving.
Kill them all and start again."

Now, God felt that Jonah should be willing to give even *bad* people a second chance. "After all," said God, "I'm willing to do that, why shouldn't he?"

So God made a beautiful tree. Jonah loved to snooze in the shade of the velvety leaves. Then, one day, God created a worm that nibbled every last leaf until the tree was bare.

When Jonah saw what had happened to his lovely tree he cried, "God, how could You let it die?"

God's voice was stern, "You're sad that I killed a tree, but you're willing to destroy a whole town full of people! Human beings can *think* about their sins and change their ways. That's why I'm willing to give the people of Nineveh a chance to try again."

Jonah understood. He took pity on the people, forgave them, and helped them. And the Ninevites *did* change their ways, so the city was saved.

Hillel and the Pagan

A pagan is someone who worships many gods instead of one, praying to the sun, moon, or stars; to idols, rocks, or even animals.

But two thousand years ago, from Israel, word was spreading of one true God, and so an impatient pagan visited a Jewish teacher. The pagan had heard that it took a long time to study the Torah (the laws that tell Jews how to live each day), and he said, "I'll become a Jew if you can teach me Torah while I'm standing on one foot."

The teacher was angry. "Are you making fun of me and the Torah? Go away!"

Then the pagan knocked on the door of another great Jewish teacher named Hillel. "I'll become a Jew," he repeated, "if you can teach me Torah as I'm standing on one foot."

"Of course," said Hillel, not a bit angry. "The law is this: Don't do anything to your neighbor that you don't want anybody to do to you. The other holy laws give you details about how to carry out that most important rule. Now," he told the man, "why don't you go and study?"

The pagan did, and he became a Jew thanks to Hillel, one of the most beloved Jewish teachers.

A Father's Advice

*A*N old Jewish father had just one son, who was the sultan's favorite servant.

Before the father died he whispered to the son, "Here's my advice. If you pass a synagogue and hear people praying, go in and pray with them." With that, the old man died.

The son stayed home and mourned for seven days.

While he was away, the vizier (the sultan's adviser) told the sultan that the boy was trying to poison him. (You see, the vizier was jealous, because the sultan trusted this boy.)

The angry sultan rode out to the ovens where they baked the pottery, and said to the potter, "Tomorrow morning, someone will come from my palace. Promise me that you'll push him into the hot oven!"

The sultan returned to the palace and told the boy, "Tomorrow, first thing, go to the pottery ovens. Tell the potter, 'Don't forget the promise you made to the sultan.'"

So next morning, the boy rode toward the ovens. He was

almost there when he passed a synagogue and heard people praying.

"I'll pray with the others," thought the young man. "I'll follow my father's advice, and then I'll deliver the sultan's message."

Meanwhile the vizier, eager to see the young man put to death, hurried to the ovens and arrived *before* the young man, who was still praying in the synagogue.

The vizier didn't see the boy anywhere, so he asked the potter, "Did you remember the promise you made to the sultan?"

Hearing that, the potter immediately pushed the vizier into the hot oven, and that was the end of him!

When the boy heard what had happened, he rushed to tell the sultan, who said, "I believed the vizier when he said you were trying to kill me. Now *he* has been punished for his lies. If you'll forgive me, I'll never doubt you again."

The boy forgave the sultan, and never forgot how his father's advice had saved his life.

31

The Cobbler from Chelm in the Big City

A cobbler from the town of Chelm grew tired while hiking to the famous city of Warsaw. But he was afraid to nap. "The road looks the same in both directions," he thought. "When I awaken, I won't know which way to walk." So he took off his boots, and pointed the *toes* toward Warsaw, and the *heels* toward Chelm. Now he would know he should follow his toes toward the big city.

But while he lay snoring, a branch dangling off the side of a wagon bumped his boots and turned them around. Now the *heels* pointed toward Warsaw and the *toes* pointed toward his hometown of Chelm.

So! When the poor cobbler awoke, he followed his toes—you guessed it! Straight back to Chelm!

"Why is Warsaw so famous?" he wondered as he wandered through the synagogue and shops in the marketplace. "This is no different from Chelm."

He discovered a stone cottage similar to his own house in every detail, and in it, a smiling woman with six chubby daughters—all looking exactly like his own family!

And since this woman and her children welcomed him as if he were the man of the house, he thought, "The real Warsaw husband must be my twin. I'll stay here till he returns, for surely I must meet him!"

And as far as is known, that's where he stayed for the rest of his days!

Praying with a Flute

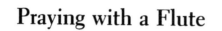

A shepherd boy could play his homemade flute more sweetly than any bird could sing. Unfortunately, the boy was quite simple and couldn't learn to read or write. As he sat in the synagogue with his father on Yom Kippur, the holiest day of the year, he couldn't understand the prayers. Soon tears filled his eyes. He wanted to pray to God, but how?

Before his father could stop him, the shepherd pulled his flute from his coat pocket and filled the synagogue with music. The congregation couldn't believe their ears. A flute, played on a serious holiday like Yom Kippur? The boy's father was terribly ashamed of his son. Traditional Jews *never* play music on Yom Kippur.

But the rabbi smiled and said, "God will hear us no matter how we pray, as long as we are truthful. This simple boy's unspoken prayer—his music—is even truer and more beautiful than ours. We pray with words from a book, yet he prayed from his heart!"

And from that night on, the shepherd boy played his flute at services, and it is said that God was delighted too!

The Good Friends
and the King

7WO friends, Eliphalet and Gideon, always studied Torah together. When they grew up, they moved to cities far from each other.

One day Gideon set out for the place Eliphalet lived to see his friend, but at the gates of the city he was arrested by police. They said Gideon was a spy, and took him to be hanged.

"I am innocent," Gideon said. "But I ask one favor," he begged the king. "Give me a week to go home and say goodbye to my family. On my word as a Jew, I swear to return."

The king sneered, "Who will guarantee that you'll come back?"

Eliphalet pushed through the crowd. "Sire, I will vouch for him. Put *me* in prison, and allow this man to visit his family. If he doesn't return, hang me instead."

The king was astonished, but he agreed.

At home, Gideon said farewell to his wife and children, and hurried back to the city where he was to die.

Everyone had gathered, for nobody expected Gideon to return. Eliphalet's neck was in the noose when there was a loud cry. "Wait! Don't hurt my friend. I am here to take his place!"

Gideon pushed through the crowd in order to save his friend.

The king was so touched by the honesty and loyalty shown by these Jewish men that he said, "In the name of friendship, I will pardon the crime of this stranger. And I only ask one favor of you—allow me to become a third friend to the two of you!"

The Horse Who Brought Home a Treasure

A poor family owned nothing but a cart and a horse so old it could hardly pull the cartful of firewood to market, which is how the family earned their money.

The father, a religious man, read the Torah to his children when they were sad and when they were hungry, and that would make them feel happy and full.

One day a thief stole the horse and cart. "What will we do now?" the children cried. "We're hungry and we have no way of earning money. We'll have to beg for charity." But the father calmly read aloud from the Torah, and soon the family had forgotten about their empty stomachs.

In the forest, the thief loaded firewood into the cart. Then he began to chop down a tree. Through a hole he chopped in the trunk, he saw, hidden away, a chestful of gold coins.

As he loaded the chest onto the cart, he dropped a few of the coins. And when the thief bent down to pick them up, the tree, which had been chopped halfway through, fell on top of him, killing him at once!

The horse waited, but when it grew hungry it walked home, as it had done every day for years.

"Our horse is back!" cried the mother.

"And it's brought us a chestful of gold coins," chanted the children. "We're rich!"

The father just smiled, because now, instead of *asking* for charity, he could *give* it to others.

And the horse was given a fine stable and plenty of food for the rest of his days.

The Honored Garment

AZARIAH and his wife were poor, but not unhappy, for they were kind, honest, and respected by their neighbors.

When their son was born, everyone brought gifts. A relative sent them a few yards of the most expensive and beautiful material in the world. The wife locked it away and said, "When my son is a man, I will send him out into the world in a wonderful robe made of this material."

The baby grew into a sweet and smart boy, but because they were poor, he was always dressed in ragged clothing.

One day a rich merchant invited everyone in town to a feast. Among the guests was Azariah's son, now grown. But nobody made room for him at the table, nor did they invite him to eat. Feeling rejected, the boy went home and told his mother what had happened.

"Don't be unhappy," said his mother. "Wait, and I'll finish a robe I am making for you that is so beautiful, everyone will bow down to you."

So the mother finished the robe she was making from the material they had received when the boy was born.

The boy went back to the feast, now dressed in the finest of robes. And as soon as the rich man saw him he got up, bowed before the boy, and said, "Come sit beside me, and eat and drink as much as you like."

The boy sat, took off his magnificent robe, and held the robe over the food. "Eat, robe," he said. "Eat all you want."

Everyone was startled. The rich man asked, "Why are you talking to your robe?"

The boy replied, "The first time I came to your feast, I was dressed in tattered clothing. Then, you paid no attention to me. Nobody asked me to sit down and eat. But when I arrived in my fancy outfit, you treated me royally. That's why I told my robe to eat. It was my wonderful clothes, not me, you were happy to see. So to me, even the sweetest thing on your table tastes bitter."

At that, the boy left and went back to his humble but proud home, and the rich man was ashamed, for he knew that the boy was right.

The Wise King

A queen had to decide which of her seven sons was worthy of becoming king when she died, so she said, "Whoever brings me the most valuable gift will become king."

A year later, the seven princes showered the queen with glorious gifts of silk robes, silver shoes, jewels, perfumes, and big black stallions.

But the youngest prince sat in the corner, ashamed to present his gift. Finally, holding the tiny hand of a frail peasant girl, he walked toward his mother.

"This child has been beaten, starved, and left all alone. She is my gift, for you to care for and love. But I am afraid this sad little girl cannot compare with the royal treasures my brothers have brought you."

The queen's eyes filled with joyous tears. "Love is the greatest treasure of all!" she said. "I choose your gift, for you have made *two* people happy. Not only does this little girl need to be cared for, but I have never had a daughter to love, and I shall raise her as my very own."

And with that, the queen placed her crown on this wise son's head, saying, "You shall not have to wait for me to die before you become king. With your wisdom and kindness, you'll make our kingdom a happy one."

And he did.

What Herschel's Father Did

The Jews were picked on and persecuted by
many people, and the Herschel tales tell
how many Jews managed to survive battles
through their sense of humor. Herschel
of Ostropol was a real person, known for
his sense of humor. Famous in Jewish folklore, he was born in the Ukraine two hundred
years ago, and his jokes and tricks are still
remembered today.

*H*erschel was hungry, so he asked an innkeeper for a bite
of food. The innkeeper could see that Herschel had no
money, so he said, "There's no food left."

"Just a crust of bread?" begged Herschel.

"Not a crumb," replied the innkeeper.

"All right, but if I don't get something to eat," Herschel
muttered to himself furiously, "if I don't get anything to eat,
I'll do exactly what my father did." And with that, Herschel

shook the innkeeper by the shoulders till his hat flew across the room. Herschel repeated, "Without something to eat, I'll do what my father did!"

The innkeeper didn't know what Herschel's father did, but he was sure that if he didn't give Herschel food, Herschel would do it to *him.*

So the innkeeper took out everything left over from dinner— the leg of a goose, bread, fruit, and tea—and served Herschel quickly, as though his life depended on it, for the innkeeper felt that it did.

Herschel ate every bit.

Then the innkeeper asked, "Now are you happy?"

"Yes, thank you," said Herschel.

"You're not angry?"

"Not at all."

"Then tell me," the innkeeper asked timidly, "what *did* your father do if he didn't get something to eat?"

Herschel smiled. "When my father didn't get anything to eat, what could he do? He went to bed hungry."

Herschel in the Woods

HERSCHEL was walking in the woods when a bandit jumped out from behind a tree, pointed a gun at him, and said, "Give me your money or I'll shoot you dead."

As Herschel handed over his little sack of coins he said, "Mr. Robber, if I arrive home without a scratch, my wife will think I spent the money and made up the story about being held up by a bandit. Please shoot a hole through my coat. That will convince her."

Herschel held out his coat, and *bang!* the thief shot a bullet right through it.

"Good enough?" he asked.

"No," said Herschel sadly, "one bullet won't do. Shoot one more through the hem." *Bang!* went the second bullet. "How about a couple more through the top of my hat?" Herschel suggested, holding his hat high in the air.

Bang! Bang!

"Now could you put one through my sleeve?" asked Herschel.

"No I can't," replied the bandit. "Sorry, but I have no more bullets," and he showed Herschel his empty gun.

"Oh," said Herschel. "Then I have something for *you.*"

And Herschel smashed the bandit over the head with a stick, knocking him to the ground. Then Herschel took back his money and went home to his loving wife.

The Perfect Books for Busy Parents!

One-Minute Stories by Shari Lewis

There's always time for reading aloud with One-Minute Stories—written and adapted by world-famous performer Shari Lewis. Parents like them because they're fast and free up time. Children like them because they're fun to memorize and retell. So take a minute and try one of the One-Minute Stories today!

19563-X **ONE-MINUTE ANIMAL STORIES** $6.95

15292-2 **ONE-MINUTE BEDTIME STORIES** $7.95

19565-6 **ONE-MINUTE BIBLE STORIES OLD TESTAMENT** $7.95

19566-4 **ONE-MINUTE BIBLE STORIES OLD TESTAMENT *** $6.95

23286-1 **ONE-MINUTE BIBLE STORIES NEW TESTAMENT**
adapted by Florence Henderson $7.95

23424-4 **ONE-MINUTE CHRISTMAS STORIES** $7.95

19322-X **ONE-MINUTE FAVORITE FAIRY TALES** $5.95

23423-6 **ONE-MINUTE GREEK MYTHS** $6.95

23425-2 **ONE-MINUTE STORIES OF BROTHERS AND SISTERS** $7.95

*Reinforced library editions.

At your local bookstore or for credit card orders of $25.00 or more, call toll-free 1-800-223-6834, Ext. 9479. In New York, please call 1-212-492-9479 and have your credit card handy. Or send your order, plus $2.00 for shipping and handling, to the address below. (Please send checks or money orders only, no cash or C.O.D.'s.)

DOUBLEDAY READERS SERVICE, DEPT. SL2
P.O. BOX 5071, DES PLAINES, IL 60017-5071

Prices and availability are subject to change without notice. Please allow four to six weeks for delivery.

A division of Bantam Doubleday Dell Publishing Group, Inc.

SL2-9/89